001

002

003

004

005

Bold Marinell of Britomart
   Is throwne on the Rich strond:
Faire Florimell of Arthur is
   Long followed, but not fond.

008

009

011

010

012

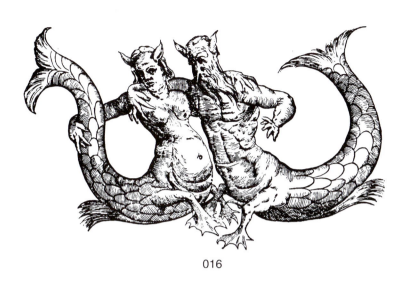

016

017

018

019

020

021

022

8

A teme of Dolphins raunged in array
Drew the smooth charett of sad Cymoent:
They were all taught by Triton to obey
To the long raynes at her commandement:

III · IV · XXXIIJ

Guyon, by Palmers governaunce,
Passing through perils great,
Doth overthrow the Bowre of blisse,
And Acrasie defeat.

027

028

029

030

031

032

033

040

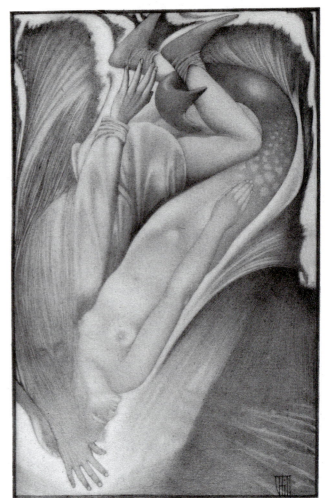

041

042

043

044

Marin, for love of Florimell,
In languor wastes his life;
The Nymph, his mother getteth her
And gives to him for wife.

047

048

049

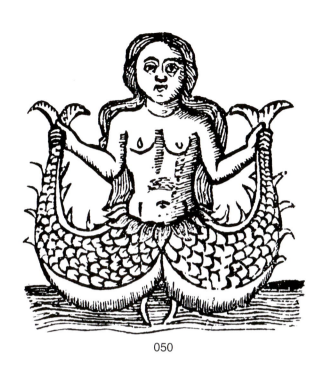

050

051

052

053

056

057

062

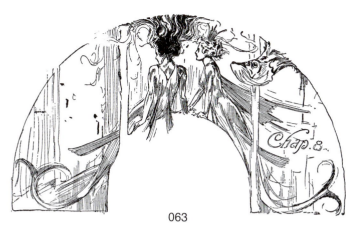
063

064

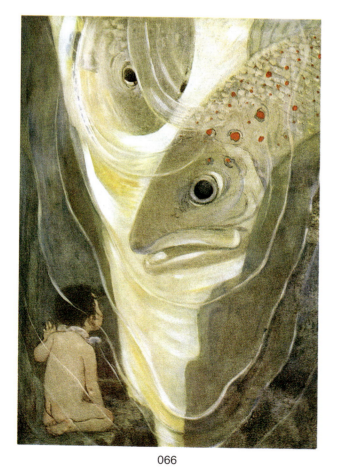
066

065

067

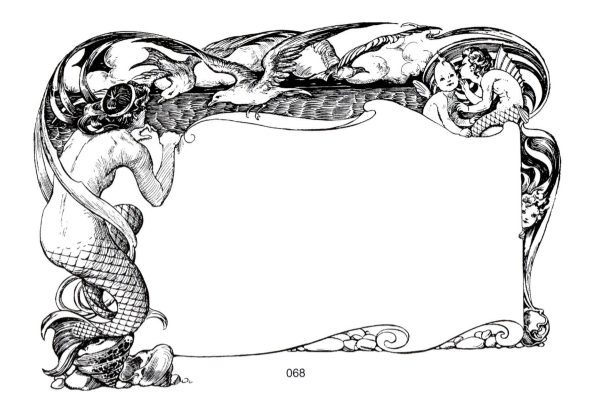
068

069

070

071

072

073

074

075

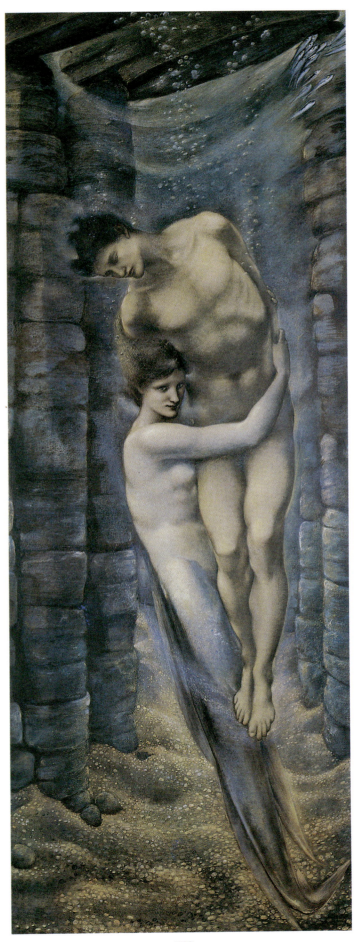
076

The Witch creates a snowy Lady
  Like to Florimell;
Who, wrong'd by Carle, by Proteus sav'd,
  Is sought by Paridell.

081

082

083

084

085

086

087

089

090

092

091

093

094

095

096
097

098

099

100

101

102

103 (insert)   104 (frame)   105 (all)

107

THE MERMAID ASKS FOR THE KING'S CHILD

108

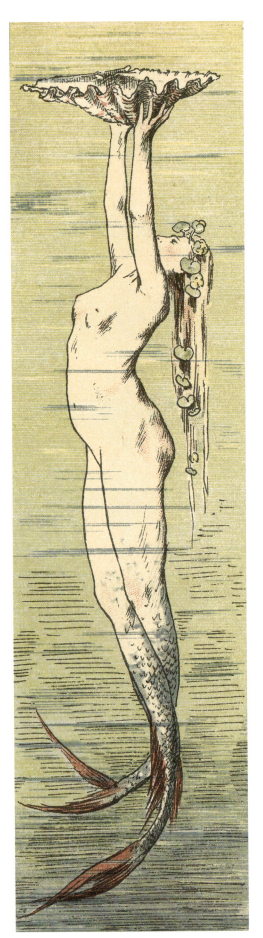

109

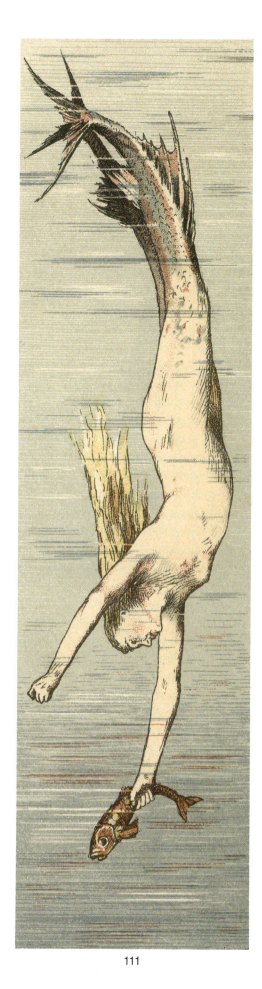

111

THE MONKEY BROUGHT TO OTOHIME

110

112

113

114

115

116

117

118

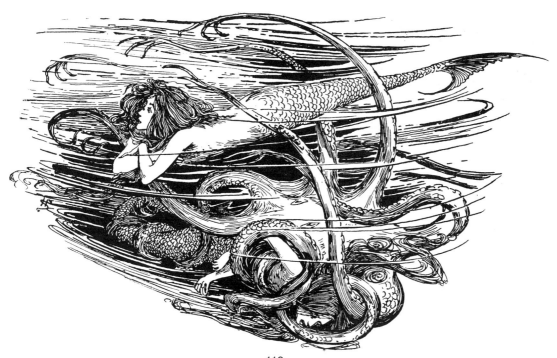

119

120

122

THE LITTLE MERMAID

123

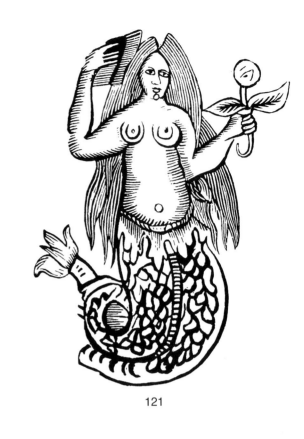

121

124

125

129

130

131

132

133

135

134

136

WHITE·AS·THE·SURF·IT·WAS·AND·LIKE·A·FLOWER·IT·TOSSED·ON·THE·WAVES

139

140

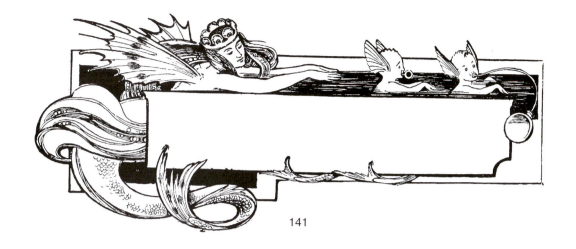

141

142